Legends of Hollywood: The L

By Charles River Editors

Publicity shot of de Havilland in 1943.

About Charles River Editors

Charles River Editors provides superior editing and original writing services across the digital publishing industry, with the expertise to create digital content for publishers across a vast range of subject matter. In addition to providing original digital content for third party publishers, we also republish civilization's greatest literary works, bringing them to new generations of readers via ebooks.

Sign up here to receive updates about free books as we publish them, and visit Our Kindle Author Page to browse today's free promotions and our most recently published Kindle titles.

Introduction

Joan Fontaine (1917-2013)

"You know, I've had a helluva life. Not just the acting part. I've flown in an international balloon race. I've piloted my own plane. I've ridden to the hounds. I've done a lot of exciting things." – Joan Fontaine

In 1939, Olivia de Havilland had her most memorable role as Melanie Hamilton in *Gone With the Wind* (1939), perhaps the most famous movie in American history, but Hollywood legend has it that she only got the role because her own younger sister, Joan Fontaine, was asked to audition for the part and recommended Olivia instead so that she could audition for Scarlett O'Hara. Although Fontaine and de Havilland would make history by becoming the only sisters to both win an Academy Award for Best Actress, that anecdote was just one of the various stories about the siblings that has shed light on their notoriously contentious and complicated relationship. As Fontaine once put it, "I married first, won the Oscar before Olivia did, and if I die first, she'll undoubtedly be livid because I beat her to it!" De Havilland herself once said, "Joan is very bright and sharp and can be cutting."

Of course, one of the reasons people have remained interested in the sisters is that both of them had such long acting careers, and Fontaine became best remembered both for a career that spanned 60 years and several high profile marriages. With typical humor, Fontaine joked about the fact she had so many husbands, commenting in jest, "If you keep marrying as I do, you learn everybody's hobby." But that attention has only served to obscure her very serious professional career, which saw her won the Oscar for Best Actress for her role in Alfred Hitchcock's *Suspicion* (1941). She also earned a nomination for her performance in *The Constant Nymph* (1943), and in a television career that spanned several decades, she earned an Emmy nomination for her work on *Ryan's Hope* in 1980, nearly 40 years after winning the Academy Award for *Suspicion*. Fontaine even appeared on Broadway in a couple of productions that ran for several years.

Legends of Hollywood: The Life of Joan Fontaine profiles the life and career of one of Hollywood's most prolific actresses. Along with pictures of important people, places, and events, you will learn about Joan Fontaine like never before, in no time at all.

Legends of Hollywood: The Life of Joan Fontaine

About Charles River Editors

Introduction

    Chapter 1: In the Shadow of the Cheery Blossoms

    Chapter 2: RKO

    Chapter 3: Rebecca and Suspicion

    Chapter 4: Established Actress

    Chapter 5: Motherhood and Melodrama

    Chapter 6: Star of Stage and Screens Big and Small

    Chapter 7: Family Feuds

    Chapter 8: Dogs at the End of the Day

    Bibliography

Chapter 1: In the Shadow of the Cheery Blossoms

"My mother, Lillian de Havilland…was beautiful, gracious and a talented actress. My father was an English professor at Waseda and Imperial universities in Tokyo who left Mother for our Japanese maid when I was 2. My mother later married a department store manager, George Milan Fontaine, but she remained the dominant figure in our lives. My family was a combination of the critical and perfectionist—and that's tough. We didn't have a loving childhood; my stepfather made sure we had a military childhood. Even our beds were khaki color. The oddest thing was that our parents had absolutely no plans for our future. You normally ask a little child, 'What do you want to be when you grow up?' We were never asked that question." – Joan Fontaine

Joan de Beauvoir de Havilland was born on October 22, 1917, just 15 months after her older sister, Olivia, and she would later joke to a journalist, "I was conceived on a chaise lounge one Saturday afternoon. Father had come home from his chess club with a moment to spare before dressing for dinner." Like her sister, Joan was born in Tokyo far away from World War I, which was still raging across Europe at the time, but she was touched by the war. Her parents gave Joan her unusual middle name in honor of a friend of theirs who was killed in battle.

Joan's father, Walter, was a member of the growing upper middle class in England. After studying at Cambridge and getting a terminal degree in English, he sought adventure in the form of taking a position as an English professor at Japan's Imperial University not long before World War I broke out. He later became an attorney specializing in Japanese patents and corporate law. Olivia's mother, Lillian, had been an aspiring actress prior to meeting her husband and had studied at the Royal Academy of Dramatic Arts in London, but she abandoned her ambitions when she and Walter moved to Japan.

The young couple had been married less than two years before Olivia was born, but there were already cracks in their fragile union by then. Walter was a notorious philanderer, even in the early years of their marriage, and by the time their second daughter Joan was born in 1917, Lillian was thoroughly discouraged with her husband and her marriage. To make matters worse, both the girls had severe asthma, and the treatments available in Japan were not helping them. Joan in particular was a sickly child after contracting measles while living in Japan, and before she had fully recovered, she developed a type of virulent streptococcal infection that left her weak and anemic.

Given the sisters' illnesses, Lillian insisted that Walter take her and the girls back to England. Her hope was that the gentler English climate would allow her daughters to make a full recovery. The trip home to England began with a ship to California, and from there the family planned to take a train across North America to board another ocean liner for England. However, by the time they arrived in California, three-year-old Olivia was very ill. Lillian explained to her husband that they needed to remain in California long enough for Olivia to recover before beginning the arduous overland journey. He agreed to leave Lillian and the girls in California, but he insisted that he must return to his law practice in Japan. He did not tell Lillian that he would also be returning to his Japanese mistress, though she was probably all too aware of that too.

Meanwhile, Lillian soon realized that California's warm, sunny climate was just what her daughters needed, so she rented a house in Saratoga, a small community about 50 miles south of San Francisco. She also allowed the girls to be given infant IQ tests designed to determine the intelligence of children before they entered pre-school or kindergarten. Three-year-old Joan surprised everyone by scoring 160, well within the genius level, on her test, but school was not a happy place for young Joan. She later remembered, "When I was a little girl unable to hold my own with those who should have been my friends…I was fearful and timid. And I lived in constant horror of criticism." It didn't help that Joan and her sister had to take diction lessons because their parents wanted them to be well-spoken. They were forced to read Shakespeare aloud each night to their mother, who popped their knuckles with a ruler if they made any mistakes. According to Fontaine, "Perfection was the least expected of us."

Lillian may have planned to live out her life in what came to be called a "Victorian divorce", in which two people would remain married but live apart, but Walter had more modern plans, so the two legally divorced in February 1925. By this time, Lillian, with her lilting English accent, had found work among California's aspiring stars teaching music and elocution. Lillian also found another husband in George Fontaine, who she married just two months after her divorce was final. Fontaine was a self-made man and the owner of a large Saratoga department store, but he did not get along with his stepdaughters, due primarily to his harsh parenting style. The girls reacted differently to his presence in their lives; Olivia drew away from him and chose to spend more time with her mother, but Joan, on the other hand, tried to win him over by pleasing him and even took his surname as her own. Differences over their parents planted the seeds of resentment and animosity that would bloom into full-fledged dislike between the two siblings as they grew older.

Had she not been so caught up in the problems surrounding her personal life, Lillian might have known that mounting hostility was developing between her two daughters. Fontaine would later tell a reporter, "I regret that I remember not one act of kindness from Olivia all through my childhood. One of my earliest memories is when she was 6 and I was 5. She had learned to read and, one night when we were alone, she read aloud the Crucifixion from the Bible with mounting gusto until finally I screamed. Olivia loved it…Olivia so hated the idea of having a sibling that she wouldn't go near my crib. She was always a stout believer in primogeniture."

The sibling rivalry continued to grow along with the girls. Joan recalled that when her sister was 9, Olivia learned about last wills and testaments and decided to make one of her own. Picking on her younger sister, she wrote, "I bequeath all my beauty to my younger sister Joan, since she has none." Mean jokes aside, at that point it seemed that young Joan might have been the one who needed a will. She would later remember, "There was always something wrong with me. For a while I averaged about two days a week in school. I had headaches, I had all kinds of pains. I was kept away from other children, never allowed to do the things they did."

On top of these problems, Joan also began having problems with her stepfather. After trying so hard to get him to like her, Joan alleged that George began making sexual advances toward her. Feeling unable to tell her mother what was going on, Joan opted to run away, causing even more distance between her and the rest of the family.

As the girls grew older, the rift between them expanded, sometimes erupting into violence. Joan wrote in her memoirs, "One July day in 1933 when I was 16, Olivia threw me down in a rage, jumped on top of me and fractured my collarbone. One person called our relationship paranoid—but he didn't say on whose part. Not mine, though I may have a persecution complex. There must be some explanation." Not long after this incident, 16 year old Joan left the United States and moved back to Japan to live with her father, where she graduated from the American School in 1935. Fontaine's sheltered life style certainly changed her perspective on much of the history of the early 20th century; when asked about her life during the Great Depression, all she could say was, "I was in school, so I wasn't exposed during that time. And in the U.S., I was working, so again I wasn't exposed to the hard times that so many were experiencing."

Chapter 2: RKO

"I am proud that I have carved my path on earth almost entirely by my own efforts, proud that I have compromised in my career only when I had no other recourse, when financial or contractual commitments dictated. Proud that I have never been involved in a physical liaison unless I was deeply attracted or in love. Proud that, whatever my worldly goods may be, they have been achieved by my own labors." – Joan Fontaine

Not long after her graduation, Joan returned to America and learned that her older sister was pursuing an acting career. Joan decided to follow her, and she appeared for the first time on stage in 1935 in an off-Broadway production of *Kind Lady*, opposite May Robson. However, Lillian did not want her younger daughter competing with Olivia and thus refused to allow Joan to use her legal name in pictures. Joan explained, "Professionally de Havilland was Olivia's; she was the first-born and I was not to disgrace her name. I took my first theatrical name, Joan Burfield, from Burfield Street in Hollywood. Then I became Joan St. John. One evening at the Trocadero nightclub, at the urging of a fortune teller, I picked Fontaine, my stepfather's name. 'Take that,' she advised, 'Joan Fontaine is a success name.' She was right."

A picture of Olivia de Havilland in 1933.

When Fontaine appeared in a stage production of *Call It a Day* (1935), her performance impressed a talent scout from RKO, and he quickly signed her to a contract with his studio. She initially used the name Joan Burfield on the screen, and she made her first picture for the company that year, playing a small role in the big screen production of *No More Ladies* (1935). It's somewhat surprising that she was allowed to use her Christian name in the movie since the star was another Joan, and Joan Crawford at that, but Fontaine's role was so small as to be unnoticed by most of these seeing the film. In fact, like most actresses of her generation, Fontaine would spend the first few years of her career playing bit parts in big pictures, including *A Million to One* (1937) and *Quality Street* (1937).

Much to Fontaine's aggravation and disappointment, Olivia was cast in the lead of the movie version of her first play, *Call It a Day* (1937). She would later complain, "In our family Olivia was always the breadwinner, and I the no-talent, no-future little sister not good for much more than paying her share of the rent." But Joan was determined to become a star and gain the upper-hand in their long term sibling rivalry, so she threw herself into her first leading role, that of Nurse Doris King in *The Man Who Found Himself (1937)*. Fortunately, RKO was just as committed to cultivating her career; the company included extra photographs of Fontaine at the end of the credits just to make sure that everyone in the audience knew their new star's name. She received good reviews for her role, but some she certainly liked less than others, such as this one from the *New York Daily Mail*: "Miss Fontaine is as blonde as Miss de Havilland is dark, but she has the same charm and poise which makes her sister one of the most promising younger actresses in Hollywood."

By this point, the press was also taking note of the sibling rivalry. In a piece that appeared in August 1937, de Havilland was quoted as saying, "It gets to be automatic, almost… when I hear Joan slam-banking around in the shower I know it's my cue to be cheerful and pleasant. When Joan sees me come down stairs looking as though I'd like to kick the cat, she has to turn on the good nature even if it nearly kills her. Temperament just can't hold up long under such a system…We've practiced long enough now…to just about know how long one of us will be out of sorts and what the limit is to a streak of good nature in the other. We think that we change about every three days."

More determined than ever to succeed, Fontaine pressed on, making *You Can't Beat Love* (1937) and *Music for Madame* (1937). Next, she was cast opposite Fred Astaire in the musical comedy *A Damsel in Distress* (1937), even though Fontaine could not dance. Disappointed at not having his usual partner, Ginger Rogers, with him, Astaire wanted to replace Fontaine with someone else, but RKO convinced him to try to work with her. For her part, Fontaine discussed her inability to dance frankly, recalling, "I tripped over fences and stepping stones to the tune of 'Things Are Looking Up.' George and Ira Gershwin also wrote the haunting 'Foggy Day in London Town' for our film. I also fell on my face."

Perhaps not surprisingly, the results were disastrous, with the high budget film losing money at the box office, and at least one critic pointed to the movie's primary flaw: "As for 19-year-old Joan Fontaine, she's quite lovely and charming, and Astaire does his very best to camouflage her utter lack of terpsichorean ability." Fontaine would later assert that this role set her career back 4 years.

As if that wasn't bad enough, 1937 proved to be a very important year in Fontaine's life for another reason, as she would later tell a reporter: "Conrad Nagel, the actor, and I were staying with friends in northern California on our way to a duck hunt. He visited my room one night to fix the toilet, drew up a chair and sat by my bed. Suddenly he threw back the covers and, before I could protest, the dire deed was done. I was surprised out of my virginity at 20." She also wrote in her memoirs that the encounter reminded her "of when I had to stand up in class as a child and be vaccinated."

Nagel

For a time it looked like Fontaine's career would end before it started. She made seven more movies in 1938 and 1939, but only one of them, *The Women* (1939), was memorable, and that's because it featured some of the best actresses of the day, including Joan Crawford, Rosalind Russell, Norma Shearer and Paulette Godard. While Fontaine was barely noteworthy at the time, the lessons that she learned working with them would influence the rest of her professional life, and she would also be remembered for outliving all her other cast members. She recalled, "I learned about acting from George [Cukor] than anyone else and through just one sentence. He said, 'Think and feel and the rest will take care of itself.'"

Fontaine in the trailer for *The Women*.

Fontaine's work in *The Women* was not enough to keep her with RKO, and she would later complain that the reason she was terminated was because she would not sleep with the right people. Whether that was accurate or sour grapes, when her contract with RKO expired, the company chose not to renew it, and for the first time in her career, Fontaine was on her own.

While she might have been alone professionally, her personal life was a different matter. In 1939, she married actor Brian Aherne, but the marriage seems to have been doomed from the start. The night before their wedding, he asked a friend to call Fontaine and tell her that he didn't think he could go through with it. She sent word back to him that it was too late to back out, but that if they were unhappy together she would give him a divorce later. With such a start, it is not surprising that their union would end just six short years later. For her part at least, Fontaine seemed to want to make her marriage work. She told a reporter interviewing her at that time, "Too many Hollywood marriages have smashed up because husbands were Mr. Joan Fontaine. That will never happen in our marriage because I am 100% Mrs. Brian Aherne." Fontaine was still just 21 years old and at the beginning of what she expected to be a long, successful career. At the same time, audiences would also like to believe that her life was as enchanted and romantic as those of the people she played on screen, so no matter what her true feelings might be, she seemed determined to give the impression that she was the happy young wife who just happened to also be a rising actress.

Aherne

Chapter 3: Rebecca and Suspicion

"Rebecca is a fantastic story, marvelously directed and produced…and although Suspicion isn't a classic like Rebecca, its damn good." – Joan Fontaine

Fontaine had been treading water professionally for the past few years, but fortunately for her, David O. Selznick was looking for a chance to follow-up the previous year's success of *Gone With The Wind* with another "made from novel" movie. This time, the book was *Rebecca*, by Daphne du Maurier, and as fate would have it, Joan was seated next to Selznick at a dinner party one night. After telling her about his plans for the film, he invited her to audition for the lead, thinking that the 22 year old Fontaine would be an excellent choice for the naïve second-wife of the mysterious Mr. DeWinter. She later discussed the process: "I made about seven tests for 'Rebecca'. Everybody tested for it. Loretta Young, Margaret Sullivan, Vivien Leigh, Susan Hayward, Anne Baxter, you name her. Supposedly, Hitchcock saw one of my tests and said, 'This is the only one'. I think the word he used to describe what set me apart was 'vulnerability'. Also, I was not very well-known and producer David O. Selznick saw the chance for star-budding. And may I say he also saw the chance to put me under contract for serf's wages."

Selznick

At this time, Alfred Hitchcock was still relatively unknown to Americans, and since *Rebecca* (1940) would be his first American film, he was determined to make it great. He cast Fontaine opposite British heartthrob Laurence Olivier, which proved to be a bit of a problem: "Hitch and I got along quite well. He was what they call an 'actor's director'. At the time, Olivier was engaged to Vivien Leigh and he wanted her to play my role. Hitch came to me the first week of shooting and told me that Olivier said that I was awful and that Vivien was the only one that should play opposite him. To be so young and to be handed that kind of information! I kept my head down and did my work and although I couldn't stand Larry for saying that, I don't think it ever showed."

Famous for holding a grudge, Fontaine would complain a decade later, "The cast were all British and a cliquey bunch. They didn't include me in anything. No chats off set, mind you. It made me so nervous that it affected the way I approached the role I played. I was on edge all the time during the filming because I could feel their dislike towards me. It was positively palpable. Hitch never interceded on my behalf. But genius that he was, he allowed it to continue and because of that I stayed in this very tense state while filming and that is just what the role called for."

To fans of Alfred Hitchcock's later work, *Rebecca* is a surprising and perhaps disappointing film, since it does not contain the many qualities that would make Hitchcock a box office favorite. There is none of the dark comedy that peppers films such as *To Catch a Thief* (1953) or *North by Northwest* (1959), and Laurence Olivier's demeanor is a bit stiffer than what one finds with Cary Grant or James Stewart, the actors most commonly identified with Hitchcock. However, *Rebecca* is every bit as suspenseful as Hitchcock's later movies. The gothic plot involves a marriage between Maxim (Olivier) and an anonymous woman (Joan Fontaine). The two meet while Maxim is on vacation, and they are from vastly different backgrounds - the wealthy Maxim is sharply juxtaposed against Fontaine's working-class status. As with other films of the genre, there is an age discrepancy between Maxim and Fontaine's character, because even though Olivier was just 10 years older than Fontaine, he appears old enough to be her father. Eventually, it is revealed that Rebecca replaces Maxim's first wife only to find herself tormented by her husband's maid, who repeatedly indicates that Fontaine will never measure up to her predecessor. It is also revealed that Rebecca was herself a dishonorable woman. Having uncovered the mysteries of the past, Olivier and Fontaine embark on a fresh life together.

Publicity studio shot of Hitchcock.

Fontaine and Judith Anderson in *Rebecca*.

Cast resentments aside, Hitchcock's decisions proved to be the right ones. In addition to making $4.5 million, *Rebecca* was showered with Academy Award nominations. It won the Oscar for Best Picture and Best Cinematography and was nominated for nine others. Among these, Olivier was nominated for Best Actor, Fontaine for Best Actress, and Hitchcock for Best Director (an award that the famous director would never win, at least not until being presented with an Honorary Oscar in 1968). According to one critic, "Miss Fontaine is excellent as the second wife, carrying through the transition of a sweet and vivacious bride to that of a bewildered woman marked by the former tragedy she finds hard to understand." Another observed, "Miss Du Maurier never really convinced me any one could behave quite as the second Mrs. de Winter behaved and still be sweet, modest, attractive and alive. But Miss Fontaine does it not simply with her eyes, her mouth, her hands and her words, but with her spine. Possibly it's unethical to criticize performances anatomically. Still we insist Miss Fontaine has the most expressive spine — and shoulders we've bothered to notice this season."

In addition to her first Academy Award nomination for Best Actress, Fontaine also came in third in the New York Film Critics Circle Award for Best Actress. When *Rebecca* was made into a radio play and broadcast on *Screen Guild Theater* three years later, Fontaine reprised her role, but this time her leading man was her own husband, Brian Ahern.

While she did not win the Oscar, Fontaine did win Hitchcock's respect, and with that, she got the lead in his next movie, *Suspicion (1941)*. *Suspicion* starred Joan Fontaine as Lina, a shy woman from a wealthy background who marries an older man named Johnnie (played by Cary Grant). The marriage is a study in contrasts; Grant's character has an irresponsible background, while Fontaine is far more prudish. In the film, the marriage is not one of mutual love so much as the fact that Grant represented the polar opposite of Fontaine's father, thus continuing a long line of Freud-inspired Hollywood films that saw the husband as a replacement for the woman's father. Fontaine suspects that her husband is plotting to kill her for her life insurance, and the film reaches a dramatic conclusion when Grant takes her for a dangerous car ride while speeding along tortuous roads, but he prevents his wife from falling out of the car when her door inadvertently opens.

The film prepares the viewer for an actual murder, and the happy ending feels forced, but the drama of the plot compensates for the tacked-on ending and the film is still possible to enjoy. Nevertheless, Hitchcock was deeply critical of the ending when discussing the film later in life: "Well, I'm not too pleased with the way *Suspicion* ends. I had something else in mind. The scene I wanted, but it was never shot, was for Cary Grant to bring her [Fontaine] a glass of milk that's been poisoned and Joan Fontaine has just finished a letter to her mother…She drinks the milk and dies. Fade out and fade in on one short shot: Cary Grant, whistling cheerfully, walks over to the mailbox and pops the letter [referring to Lina's life insurance policy] in." While this ending would certainly have been less superficial than the one that Hitchcock was forced to use, it is not difficult to see why he was forced to switch endings; by 1941, Cary Grant was one of the premier actors in Hollywood, and it wouldn't have been good for his image if his character performed an act as evil as murdering his own spouse.

Fontaine's experience with Grant was completely different than with Olivier, in part because they had worked together a few years earlier in *Gunga Din* (1939) and were thus familiar with each other. However, the ending caused some problems for Grant, as Fontaine noted, "Working with Cary Grant was wonderful, but I think he wanted a departure from all those light comedies he had been doing. He saw 'Suspicion' as his great dramatic role. He did kill me in the original cut, but at the preview, the audience simply refused to accept him as the murderer…Halfway through the filming, Cary realized that the whole picture was being told through the eyes of the woman, which gave him quite a shock, since he had given his approval to my being cast on the assumption that he would get to kill me…"

Whatever his concerns about his role, the chemistry between Grant and Fontaine impressed plenty of critics, and according to the review in *Variety*, "Joan Fontaine successfully transposes to the screen her innermost emotions and fears over the wastrel and apparently-murderous antics of her husband. Cary Grant turns in a sparkling characterization as the bounder who continually discounts financial responsibilities and finally gets jammed over thefts from his employer."

Fontaine in the trailer for Suspicion.

Suspicion was nominated for an Academy Award for Best Picture and Best Score, but most importantly for Fontaine, she was nominated for Best Actress. However, there was a very personal complication to Fontaine's nomination this time because her sister had also been nominated for an Oscar for Best Actress. When Fontaine won the Oscar over her sister, de Havilland seemed to be gracious in defeat by offering her a congratulatory handshake at the ceremony, but Joan snubbed her attempt. This enraged Olivia, who not only had to deal with that slight but also the fact that her younger sister had just won acting's most prestigious award before she had. Fontaine would later explain the emotions behind her actions that night: "I froze. I stared across the table, where Olivia was sitting. 'Get up there!' she whispered commandingly. Now what had I done? All the animus we'd felt toward each other as children, the hair-pullings, the savage wrestling matches, the time Olivia fractured my collarbone, all came rushing back in kaleidoscopic imagery. My paralysis was total. I felt Olivia would spring across the table and grab me by the hair. I felt age 4, being confronted by my older sister. Damn it, I'd incurred her wrath again!"

Fontaine and Gary Cooper at the Academy Awards in 1942.

Publicity shot of de Havilland in the 1940s.

Joan's success may have added to the sibling rivalry, but it also fueled de Havilland professionally, because the Oscar loss marked a turning point in her perspective. Olivia later admitted that she stopped believing in God for a few weeks after losing to her sister, and she also explained how it spurred her to make changes: "So I realized that at Warners I was never going to have the work that I so much wanted to have. After Melanie and Hold Back the Dawn... Jack would cast me in an indifferent film and an indifferent role, and I thought, 'I'll have to refuse, I must do it,' and I did, and of course, I was put on suspension. Now, the contracts allowed that in those days. If you said, 'No, I don't want to do this part,' they would then suspend the contract for the length of time it took another actress to play the role, and they would take that period of time, tack it on to the end of the contract. So in May of 1943, I found myself with six months of suspension time."

When de Havilland won her own Oscar for *To Each His Own*, she went out of her way to brush past Fontaine's outstretched hand of congratulations. De Havilland complained to her agent about Fontaine's attempt to congratulate her, "I don't know why she does that when she knows how I feel." *Variety* wrote about the scene, "Joan stood there looking after her with a bewildered expression and then shrugged her shoulders and walked off." Joan described the incident, "She took one look at me, ignored my hand, clutched her Oscar and wheeled away." It certainly didn't help that by this time, there had been yet another argument between them when de Havilland learned what Fontaine had said of her new husband, novelist Marcus Goodrich: "All I know about him is that he has had four wives and has written one book. Too bad it isn't the other way around."

In spite of their differences, or perhaps because of them, Fontaine and de Havilland remain the only two siblings to win Academy Awards for acting leads, an irony not lost on Fontaine: "…neither of us [sees the other's pictures] because there are certain family traits that are too close. We would become too self-conscious. By the way, we may not get along personally, but I am absolutely thrilled that my sister has accomplished what she has. Imagine what we could have done if we had gotten together. We could have selected the right scripts, the right directors, the right producers—we could have built our own empire. But it was not to be."

Chapter 4: Established Actress

"Those days were fantastic in Hollywood because the war was beginning. All the great artists from Europe were coming to us because many of them were Jewish, many of them were persecuted one way of another of another in Europe, so we got them. We also got a lot of people that would have been in the south of France in the Scott Fitzgerald Era, Cole Porter and Barbara Hutton, all those people. They came to Hollywood, too. So we had a mélange of the most exciting, special people. And so I am spoiled for the rest of my life because of that." – Joan Fontaine

Fontaine would later complain about the changes that her Oscar win brought to her personal life, telling one journalist, "We were all actors doing a job. Everyone was professional. I respected them and they gave me respect. After the Oscar, things did change, they seemed intimidated." Not long after *Suspicion* was released, Fontaine was invited to place her hand and foot prints in front of the highly prestigious Grauman's Chinese Theatre. She appeared there on May 26, 1942, performing the rite of passage in front of dozens of flashing cameras. She also signed her name with a flourish before daintily excusing herself to wash her hands.

Of course, with two Oscar nominations and one win under her belt, Fontaine quickly found herself being cast in some of the best movies being made during World War II. She received her third Oscar nomination for her role in *The Constant Nymph* (1943), appearing opposite Charles Boyer in *The Constant Nymph*. She would later call him "my favorite leading man," adding, "I found him a man of intellect, taste and discernment. He was unselfish, dedicated to his work. Above all, he cared about the quality of the film he was making, and unlike most leading men I have worked with, the single exception being Fred Astaire, his first concern was the film, not himself."

Fontaine received her third Oscar nomination for *The Constant Nymph*, and though she did not win the award, the movie itself was one of her favorites. However, the critics were not as crazy about the picture as she was, with one writing, "[A] major portion of excess footage is on the front end, where 40 minutes is consumed in setting up detailed background for the final event, which is a love triangle, with Charles Boyer the focal point for conflict between teenager played by Joan Fontaine and the older Alexis Smith. The stretch hits yawning periods."

Boyer

Fontaine found the war years to be the busiest of her young life. Not only was she making movies, but she volunteered as often as she could at the famous Hollywood Canteen. She even worked as a nurse's aide at the local hospital, freeing trained nurses to serve in military and field units. She later wrote about one humorous incident that left her husband incredibly embarrassed: "During a trip under the aegis of a British War Relief campaign we were at the Mormon temple in Salt Lake City. It happened to be the anniversary of a college sorority and all the girls celebrated by coming to meet the handsome actor. Microphones were thrust in front of us. Brian was to deliver a message to the RAF pilots who would be listening to a shortwave rebroadcast. Did have to anything in particular to say to these brave airmen? Brian said yes indeed, he did. 'Chaps, keep your peckers up!' Silence...the girls fled in embarrassment. The president minister blanched. Only when I got my English husband back to our hotel did I inform him that in

America 'pecker' did not mean 'chin.'"

Though she grew up in the United States and had never spent a day in Great Britain, Fontaine was still considered a British subject, and the issue of her citizenship and residency became more complex as World War II wore on. If England was conquered, the triumphant Nazis could demand that all British citizens be sent home. On the off chance that such a thing could happen, Fontaine became a naturalized American citizen, but that didn't change much in her career. "The parts I was given were for a British 'lady'. I was cast because I was a young British actress. After becoming an American citizen, really nothing changed. By that time I was established."

Ironically, she was naturalized the same year that she starred in a movie based on a quintessentially English novel. She did not enjoy making *Jane Eyre* (1943), in which she played the governess turned love interest of a wealthy man, and part of the problem was that she found her co-star, Orson Welles, difficult to work with: "You cannot battle an elephant. Orson was such a big man in every way that no one could stand up to him. On the first day at 4 o'clock, he strode in followed by his agent, a dwarf, his valet and a whole entourage. Approaching us, he proclaimed, 'All right, everybody turn to page eight.' And we did it, though he was not the director." She also didn't care for the feedback she received from her mother about her performance: "She told a friend of hers that in *Jane Eyre* 'Joan was defeated by her beauty.' How's that for a remark? Mother never could express pride in either of her daughters."

Fontaine in the trailer for Jane Eyre.

Still under contract with Selznick, Fontaine next made *Frenchman's Creek* (1944), based on Daphne du Maurier's pirate tale set in 17th century France. Though there was a lot of money invested in the picture, as well as beautifully constructed costumes and sets, Fontaine did not like working with the director, Mitchell Leisen.

Fontaine then tried her hand at comedy in her next picture, *The Affairs of Susan* (1945), and fans accustomed to seeing her play serious roles were surprised at how funny she could actually be. The critics were surprised too, with one observing, "Fontaine's sparkle in this first comedienne role is impressive. She swings easily from plain Jane to the seasoned actress type, then to the glamorous, and finally to the intellectual."

In the meantime, Fontaine was also making big changes in her personal life. In 1945, she and Aherne finally ended their troubled marriage, and Fontaine wrote about why she believed everything went wrong: "My actor-husband had never been an Oscar contender. A picture taken after the (Academy Award) banquet of Brian sitting alone in the empty ballroom, feet up on a chair, my fur coat over his arm, waiting patiently for the photographers to finish with the winners, graphically illustrates the plight of a marriage when the wife is more successful than the husband." The following year, in May 1946, Fontaine and William Dozier flew to Mexico City to marry away from the Hollywood spotlight. Dozier had been an actor but by this time had turned to producing movies, and he would go on to become instrumental in producing many of the *Batman* related films and television shows. Together, they formed Rampart Productions and went on to produce *Letter From an Unknown Woman* (1948), as well as a number of other films.

It must have been a comfort to Fontaine to be happily married, because her professional life was hitting some rough patches. Her next movie, *From This Day Forward*, was panned by critics, with one writing, "Joan Fontaine is not so convincing as the other 'Saturday's child' and doesn't quite fit into the picture with a sleazy and sweaty tenement brood. Also, her genteel disposition to flirt with her half-averted eyes while a wistful smile plays about her soft lips is somewhat over-worked for the Bronx. Another observed, "But as ever when Hollywood tried to engage with everyday realities, the trade-off came in glamorization - syrupy music, Fontaine (as Stevens' wife) never looking less than a film star, and an idea of poverty that must have irritated many audiences on home ground, never mind in Europe."

Next, Fontaine appeared in *Ivy* (1947), a drama that earned her rave review as the "Queen of Mean." One critic wrote, "One more characterization like that of Ivy Lexton and Joan Fontaine will have earned permanent possession of the title 'the girl you love to hate.'...Miss Fontaine plays a monstrous female with a guile that is nothing short of frightening. Her sweet, winning personality causes three men no end of emotional torture and even wins for her the affection of some females, who presumably should have seen right into her black heart. As Ivy Lexton Miss Fontaine has sunk her teeth into a role that is nothing short of a tour de force. The script writers gallantly arranged for her to run the gamut of emotions and the wardrobe people provided a dazzling assortment of period gowns, some with a cleavage that is arresting." Still, the review was not entirely sunshine and roses, as the same critic went on to observe that "there are times when she literally chews the scenery." But despite that kind of role, and even her rivalry with de Havilland, Fontaine was so popular among her peers in Hollywood that she won the Golden Apple Award for Most Cooperative Actress in 1947.

Chapter 5: Motherhood and Melodrama

"Being a woman, I have found the road rougher than had I been born a man. Different defenses, different codes of ethics, different approaches to problems and personalities are a woman's lot. I have preferred to shun what is known as feminine wiles, the subterfuge of subtlety, reliance on tears and coquetry to shape my way. I am forthright, often blunt. I have learned to be a realist despite my romantic, emotional nature." – Joan Fontaine

Fontaine's next major picture, *Letter From an Unknown Woman* (1948), came courtesy of her husband, who cast her in the role but may have later regretted how much latitude he gave her in the picture, because the critics were not kind. One wrote, "… it cannot be stated too strongly that the picture is largely Miss Fontaine's…As the lady of deathless adoration, Miss Fontaine virtually wrings herself dry, and as the darling but fickle concert pianist, Louis Jourdan saturates the air with charm. Together they make a pleasant unit for conditioning the romantic atmosphere. No one else in the picture gets much of a chance—or counts…if you are looking for sensibility and reasonable emotion in a film, beware of this over-written 'Letter.' It will choke you with rhetoric and tommy-rot."

Fontaine once more found herself in a musical when she starred opposite Bing Crosby in *The Emperor Waltz* (1948), but she did not enjoy working with the famous singer and later complained, "Crosby wasn't very courteous to me…There was never the usual costar rapport. I was a star at that time, but he treated me like he'd never heard of me. It wasn't that he had anything against Mr. Wilder. He just didn't pay much attention to him. He told me once that he had some trouble understanding his funny accent." The director in question was the famous Billy Wilder, who preferred his actors perform their lines as written instead of how Crosby had them written. Fontaine would describe the situation in another interview: "When we were doing 'The Emperor Waltz', he would appear and say to Billy Wilder, the director and co-writer, 'These are the lines we're doing today.' And Billy would say, 'Well, I don't think so.' And so Bing would say, 'Fine, I'll be playing golf, and when you decide to shoot my lines, I'll be back.'"

Crosby

Fontaine fared better in her next role as Dee Dee Dillwood in *You Gotta Stay Happy* (1948). According to one review, "…Joan Fontaine, James Stewart and Eddie Albert…have the personality and professional know-how to keep this account of an indecisive heiress running away from her newly acquired groom bubbling along…Miss Fontaine is so charming one almost overlooks the fact that she is quite expert at light comedy." But by the time *You Gotta Stay Happy* was released, Fontaine was preparing for yet another new role: mother. Her daughter, Deborah Leslie Dozier, was born in 1948, but by that time, William had not found marriage to his liking and left Fontaine in 1949. She waited a year before filing for divorce, but when she did, she asked for full custody of Deborah. William balked, and a court case ensued that cost Fontaine what might have been her next great role. She was offered the lead in *From Here to Eternity* but felt that she could not leave California at that time and travel to the movie site in Hawaii. By the time she had won custody and her divorce was finalized in 1951, the part had been given to Deborah Kerr.

No matter what her feelings might have been about the end of her second marriage, there was one person who was happy to see Dozier out of the picture. Howard Hughes, who had once reputedly been involved Olivia de Havilland, had a crush on Fontaine that went back a decade, when they had an inauspicious meeting just before the war. Fontaine explained, "He asked me to marry him three times, but it was Olivia who loved Howard Hughes. One day she invited me to a surprise party at the Trocadero where Hughes was the host. On the dance floor, he leaned down and proposed. I was furious—no one two-timed my sister, no matter what our quarrels might be. But when I tried to warn Olivia, sparks flew. I showed her his telephone number in his own handwriting that he had given me, but she was furious at me."

Hughes

Hughes would continue to try to woo her, even giving her ex-husband a job with his own RKO studio just to keep him out of the way, but according to Fontaine, "No, I was never in love with Howard. He had no humor, no sense of joy, no vivacity. Everything had to be a 'deal.'" She would always say proudly, "I was one of the few girls pursued by Howard Hughes who never had an affair with him."

Though one critic called Fontaine's next picture, *September Affair* (1950), a "banal adventure," he nonetheless praised Fontaine as someone who "abandons herself wholly to the sweet and smiling archness of her feminine charm." *Born to Be Bad* (1950) received similarly mixed reviews, with one critic observing, "In 'Born to Be Bad,'…Joan Fontaine is demonstrating how a honey-voiced demon can have her cake and eat it too up to the point where the Production Code cries out for retribution. Unfortunately, and for this the writers of the new R.K.O. production must take most responsibility, Miss Fontaine is not nearly as fascinatingly evil as she is physically attractive in an array of gorgeously tailored gowns."

Fontaine in the trailer for *Born to Be Bad*.

 While many Hollywood actresses of the Golden Era could easily be accused of raising vapid to an art form, no could say that about Joan Fontaine. She took life seriously and expected others to do the same. She was also someone who was happy to share her good fortune with others. In 1951, not long after her divorce from Dozier was final, she traveled to Peru to attend a South American film festival, and while there, she took a tour of some Inca ruins and met the Peruvian man who cared for them. In talking with him, she learned he had a daughter that he was not able to care for, and eventually the man asked Fontaine to become the girl's legal guardian and take her back to America. Fontaine agreed and solemnly promised the parents that she would return little Martita, then 4 years old, to them when she turned 16. Fontaine would later tell a reporter that adopting Martita was the thing in her life that she was the most proud of doing.

 Martita soon settled in at Fontaine's home, joining Deborah (who was also 4) and a host of pets, and the following year, on November 12, 1952, Collier Young joined the family as Fontaine's third husband. Fontaine would remain married to him for 8 years, longer than she did any of her other husbands.

 By this time in her life, Fontaine was 35 years old with a successful career, a happy marriage, and two little girls to come home to. Many in that situation may have rested on their laurels at such a moment, but she decided to expand her acting career by taking on new challenges. For one thing, she wanted to do Shakespeare, because unlike most of her peers (especially her sister), she had never appeared in any of Shakespeare's dramas. Since there were no leads suitable for a woman her age at that time, she took a small, uncredited role in *Othello* (1952), and she was so pleased with the experience that she went on to make *Ivanhoe* (1952), staring as the lovely

Rowena.

Fontaine in *Ivanhoe*.

Fontaine continued to try to challenge herself, including playing four different roles in *Decameron Nights* (1953). She loved making that movie, which was filmed on location, as she later told one reporter, "It was wonderful to live at the Alhambra and to film all over Spain. It was glorious." She also went on to appear in *Flight to Tangier* (1953) and *The Bigamist* (1953), but she was still not satisfied. Restless and looking to try her hand at something new, Fontaine began turning her attention to other forms of entertainment.

Chapter 6: Star of Stage and Screens Big and Small

"This is the best period of my life. There are lots of offers, but going back to a sound stage in Hollywood doesn't appeal anymore. After some 50 films, I want to do things I haven't done, like appear on the London stage and write a novel. Life's too short." – Joan Fontaine

In 1954, Fontaine found the new challenge she was looking for when she took over for Deborah Kerr in the Broadway version of *Tea and Sympathy*, and while her performance was not widely considered outstanding, one critic did call it "forceful and thoughtful." She remained with the production for almost two years until June 1955 and would later tell a journalist, "I have always enjoyed stage work. You can feel the audience reactions and are able to adjust your performance accordingly."

Fontaine also made her television debut during this time by appearing in two different episodes of the TV series *Four Star Playhouse* during the 1953-54 season, playing Trudy in the episode by the same name and "The Girl on the Park Bench." She also starred opposite Bob Hope in the satirical comedy *Casanova's Big Night* (1954), but her subsequent film, *Serenade* (1956), was a box-office disaster that lost over $500,000. The dark drama *Beyond a Reasonable Doubt* did little better, and Fontaine was now forced to consider that her days as a big name star might be coming to an end.

Fontaine in *Beyond a Reasonable Doubt*.

Fontaine's film career was clearly on the decline, but she was still not quite 40 years old and wanted to keep working, so she continued to look to television and appeared in the episode "Your Other Love" with *The Ford Television Theatre* in 1956. That same year, she also appeared on *The 20th Century Fox Hour*, starring in "Stranger in the Night." Fontaine continued to make television appearances throughout the rest of the 1950s, including appearing on two episodes of *The Joseph Cotton Show*, playing a character called Adrienne in "Final Charm" and appearing in "The De Santre Story" during the 1956-57 season. She also appeared in five episodes of *General Electric Theater* between 1956 and 1960, typically playing mature women in such dramas as "The Story of Judith" and "The Victorian Chaise Lounge."

Island in the Sun (1957) was one of Fontaine's last films and by far her most controversial. The movie centered around racial tension on a tropical plantation, and most notably, the movie featured an interracial relationship between Fontaine's character and an African-American man. She would later remember, "In that picture Harry Belafonte was the most beautiful man ever. I believe he kissed me and that was shocking…I got letters from the Ku Klux Klan, I got terrible letters…the blacks…were in the back of the bus, they weren't allowed in the same restaurant with you much less to kiss you, so that was an innovation. And I am glad that it was and I'm glad things have changed." While Fontaine's performance was not popular among the film's critics, the movie itself was a box office hit that helped tear down at least some prejudicial views a few years before the Civil Rights Movement was in full swing.

Belafonte

As it turned out, *Island in the Sun* was Fontaine's last hit movie. Her next film, *Until They Sail* (1957), lost money, as did *A Certain Smile* (1958), which received several Oscar nominations but lost $1 million. Disappointed with the types of roles she was being offered, Fontaine began to work less and less. In 1959 she appeared in the *Westinghouse Desilu Playhouse* episode "Perilous", and she next appeared in 1960's *Startime* in an episode called, perhaps ironically, "Closed Set." She also appeared in *Alcoa Presents: One Step Beyond* in the eerie episode "The Visitor."

Fontaine in *Until They Sail*.

As Fontaine's film career was seemingly reaching its end, the new decade also brought an end to Fontaine's marriage. She filed for divorce from Young in November 1960, nearly 8 years to the day after their marriage, and by the time the divorce was finalized the following January, she was seeing someone new. This relationship was different, however, as she was now very quietly dating former presidential candidate and new U.S. Ambassador to the United Nations, Adlai Stevenson. She explained, "We had a tenderness for each other that grew into something rather serious. There was so much speculation about our marrying in the press that over lunch at his apartment in the Waldorf Towers he told me he could not marry an actress. He still had political ambitions and the 'little old ladies from Oshkosh' wouldn't approve. I told him it was just as well. My family would hardly approve of my marrying a politician."

Stevenson

With Stevenson clearly out of her reach, Fontaine made yet another picture. In *Voyage to the Bottom of the Sea*, she played psychiatrist Dr. Susan Hiller, who is assigned to accompany a deep sea voyage and manage any psychological problems those in the submarine might suffer. While the film did well at the box office and launched a number of follow-ups, including a television series, it brought Fontaine no particular acclaim, as her role was simply not significant enough to stand up against all the technical features the movie sported.

Undeterred, Fontaine stayed busy during 1961 by making her first made-for-TV movie, *The Light That Failed*, and she also appeared on an episode of *Checkmate* entitled "Voyage Into Fear". The following year, she turned up on *The Dick Powell Show* in an episode entitled "The Clocks", and she also starred as Baby Warren in *Tender is the Night* (1962), a box office disaster that lost more than $2 million.

In 1963, after appearing on an episode of the ever popular series *Wagon Train*, Fontaine worked one last time with her old friend Alfred Hitchcock when she appeared on his popular television show *The Alfred Hitchcock Hour*. Though it was nothing like the days they had spent making movies together, Fontaine still found it very rewarding to once more work with one of her favorite directors.

Chapter 7: Family Feuds

"When you're from a broken home, as I was, longevity in a marriage is not important. It would have been appalling to know I had to have breakfast with any one of those husbands for the rest of my life! Marriage is a love affair, and when the love affair is over, you fold your tent and away you go. But I must say, if I could have combined the good qualities of all my husbands, it would have been fantastic!" – Joan Fontaine

The stars must have aligned in an unusual manner during Christmas 1962, because it was the only holiday that Fontaine and de Havilland spent together during their adult lives, along with their husbands and children. There may have been tension in the air, but everyone made it through unscathed. As Fontaine put it, "We're getting closer together as we get older, but there would be a slight problem of temperament. In fact, it would be bigger than Hiroshima."

1963 saw Fontaine begin to back off from making films and television appearances in order to focus more of her time on her daughters, who were both 16 and beginning to get involved in some things they should not. Her main problem was with Martita. Good to her word, Fontaine had bought her a round trip plane ticket to visit her parents in Peru as soon as she turned 16, but the girl didn't want to go and ran away from home to avoid making the trip. When Fontaine finally tracked her down, she learned that the United States did not recognize her Peruvian adoption papers, and as a result, she had no control over what the girl did. Thought they would later reconcile, the two remained estranged for over 15 years, with Fontaine saying in 1978, "Until my adopted daughter goes back to see her parents, she's not welcome. I promised her parents. I do not forgive somebody who makes me break my word."

On January 23, 1964, Fontaine tried her hand one last time at marriage, this time wedding Alfred Wright, Jr., a golf editor for *Sports Illustrated*. Fontaine was an avid golfer and had even once made a hole-in-one, so the two had that in common. She also wanted another child, even though she was now 46, possibly because, like many other career focused women, she was feeling a sense of loss at having missed out on her daughters' early years. Now that her career was nearly over, another baby would give her a second chance at motherhood, but it was not meant to be. She became pregnant twice in 1964, but she miscarried both times.

While focusing on her new husband and hopes for another child, Fontaine took a break from acting. She made no movies during 1964, nor did she appear on any television shows. Her next televised appearance was in the 1965 episode "Operation Man Save" on *The Bing Crosby Show*, and she followed that with her final feature length film, *The Witches*, known in some places as *The Devil's Own*. Truth be told, the only reason she got the lead in this movie was that she was producing it herself, and as a result, her movie career would end not with a shout but with a whimper, with the movie opening to lukewarm reviews.

Also in 1964, a firestorm swept through Brentwood, California, burning Fontaine's home to the ground. She would be haunted by the fear of losing another home to fire, to the extent that another decade would pass before she bought another house. Fontaine's final break with Hollywood followed soon after when she was offered a role she just couldn't bring herself to play. After she was asked to co-star with Elvis Presley as his mother, Fontaine had reached the final straw, explaining, "Not that I had anything against Elvis Presley. But that just wasn't my cup of tea." She decided to give up filmmaking altogether and move to the East Coast, where she would focus her time and effort on theatre and television, but Fontaine's fourth husband would not be going with her. Instead, she and Wright would go their separate ways, making their divorce final in 1969.

Having been married four times, Fontaine was considered by many to be an expert on what made marriages fail, but she usually talked about her romantic life in a tongue-in-cheek manner. On one occasion, she quipped, "The main problem in marriage is that, for a man, sex is a hunger—like eating. If a man is hungry and can't get to a fancy French restaurant, he'll go to a hot dog stand. For a woman, what's important is love and romance." She also joked, "Marriage, as an institution, is as dead as the dodo bird." One question that Fontaine was often asked during the late 1960s was if she would ever marry again, but she was uninterested, telling one reporter, "I just haven't time. On two separate occasions recently men offered me $1 million if I would marry them. So I said, 'Suppose I already have $1 million? Now what will you give me?' They couldn't offer anything, not love, not a life together, not adventure—just the dough. I don't need that. I'm very good with money."

By the time her final marriage ended, Fontaine was once again working on Broadway, this time appearing in *Forty Carats*, beginning the day after Christmas 1968 and running through November 1970. While she was appearing in *Forty Carats*, her home was robbed, and she lost a number of pieces of valuable jewelry, but she joked about the incident, "All the jewelry I lost came from me. Somehow I was the kind of a girl to whom husbands — and other men, too — gave copper frying pans. I never could quite figure it out."

Fontaine would spend the rest of the 1970s touring with various traveling theatre companies. She particularly enjoyed working in Austria, where she played Eleanor of Aquitaine in *The Lion in Winter*, and she would later admit that that role gave her "the best reviews of my career." But it was also while she was on tour that the final rift occurred between her and Olivia de Havilland. When their mother fell ill and was diagnosed with cancer, de Havilland wanted her to undergo surgery in hopes that the radical treatment would save her life. Fontaine disagreed, insisting that their 88 year old mother was too old to be put through the procedure. Thinking the issue was resolved, Fontaine left town, and she later explained what happened next, "I had kept in touch with Olivia for my mother's sake, but when she was dying of cancer in California and I was touring in Cactus Flower, nobody called to say she was asking for me. Then Olivia and the executor of the estate took full charge, disposing of Mother's effects as well as her body—she was cremated—without bothering to consult me. I wasn't even invited to the memorial service.

Of course, I went anyway. At the end of it, the minister handed Olivia a box containing my mother's ashes. She scattered a handful of ashes over the grave site and then silently passed the container to me. Not one word was exchanged. I think it is so ironic that the death of this marvelous woman was responsible for our final schism." Fontaine would later add, "My sister is a very peculiar lady. When we were young, I wasn't allowed to talk to her friends. Now, I'm not allowed to talk to her children, nor are they permitted to see me. This is the nature of the lady. Doesn't bother me at all." This didn't seem to be entirely true, however, because Fontaine stopped speaking to her own daughters when she learned they were still in contact with de Havilland.

In 1975, Fontaine took time from her stage work to do a guest appearance as aging film star Thelma Cain on the popular television crime show *Cannon*. She also appeared in the made-for-TV movie *The Users* in 1978. During the years in between, she completed work on her autobiography, entitled *No Bed of Roses*, which was a forthright account that offended plenty of people from her past. Joan's former husband Brian Aherne allegedly quipped that the memoir should have been called *No Shred of Truth*.

Of course, the memoir only made the mutual disdain between Joan and her sister that much worse, and de Havilland explained why she decided to be fully estranged from Fontaine after the memoir came out: "I got that solution from reading a wonderful little agenda. Every page had a profound quotation from a saint or a philosopher, and one day I turned a page and it said: 'Avoid destructive people.' I thought, 'That's marvellous, and moral, too. If you are faced with the source of an insoluble problem, one that is useless and painful and destructive, well, avoid it.' Avoidance is a non-destructive, benevolent solution.'"

Chapter 8: Dogs at the End of the Day

"I have no illusions that age, the rigors of my profession, disappointments, and unfulfilled dreams have not left their mark." – Joan Fontaine

By the time she gave up making movies, Fontaine had enough money to live on for the rest of her life. She was a savvy business woman who had invested much of her Hollywood earnings in California real estate, so she only needed to work when she wanted to, and that was rarely the case. However, she still decided to try her hand on the afternoon soap opera *Ryan's Hope*, appearing in five episodes and giving a performance that was effective enough to earn her a Daytime Emmy nomination for Outstanding Guest/Cameo Appearance in a Daytime Drama Series. Like almost every other actor her age, she made a guest appearance on *The Love Boat* in 1981, and she also tried another soap appearance in 1983, guest starring in Hours Four and Five of the short lived drama *Bare Essence*.

Due to her age, fame and popularity, Fontaine was also frequently invited to serve on special committees related to the film industry. In 1982, she was invited to serve as the head of the jury at that year's Berlin International Film Festival. On a personal level, she was an active member of the Episcopal Actors' Guild of America, and she would go on to be one of the founding members of their George Holland Society in 1998.

With one notable exception, 1986 would mark Fontaine's last year on television, and she went out with a bang. First, she appeared in episodes of the popular nighttime dramas *Crossings* and *Hotel*, and she concluded her television career by starring in the aptly titled *Dark Mansions*. With that, she was done, content to live out the rest of her life in quiet.

At this point, Fontaine was 69, but she had come from a family tree full of women who lived long, healthy lives, and she threw herself into new pursuits, one of which was cooking. She trained at the famous Cordon Bleu cooking school and became an excellent chef. She also still flew planes, though not very often, after having earned her pilot's license years earlier. She even participated in hot air balloon races. Over the last few decades of her life, she only came out of retirement one time, starring as Queen Ludmilla in the television holiday movie *Good King Wenceslas* (1994).

Upon completing work on *Good King Wenceslas*, Fontaine purchased what would become her favorite home, and as was so often the case in her life, she obtained what she wanted because she could see what other people missed: "The husband of a newlywed couple was killed in a car accident shortly after their marriage. The bride never took possession of the house and it was put up for sale. It was overlooked by many prospective buyers because they felt their view of the ocean was obstructed by the large Cypress trees. I realized the trees could be trimmed back without losing any of their beauty and voila! View of ocean!" Located in Carmel-by-the-Sea, California, she called her new estate Villa Fontana and threw herself into gardening, developing some of the loveliest landscaping in the area. She also worked on decorating the inside of the house after having become a licensed interior decorator in her "spare time." She would live there the rest of her life, and during that time Carmel-by-the-Sea would host a growing number of Hollywood celebrities, including Clint Eastwood and Brad Pitt.

With no husband in her life, Fontaine preferred to spend her final years with four-legged friends. She became an avid supporter of the her local S.P.C.A. and made it a habit of having as many as five dogs in and around her home at all times. When one would reach the end of its life, she would quickly move on, anxious to save another dog from euthanasia. In speaking of one loss she said, "These are my dear, dear babies…We did not allow ourselves more than a day to mourn. Instead I called the S.P.C.A., and got another dog right away. We did not let ourselves cry on and on about his death. Life goes on." And yet, even her love for animals was tinged by her unresolved feelings about her family: "Animals, all kinds, are one's friends. As a child, Mother never allowed me to have pets. As an adult I found them to be loyal friends." She also told one reporter that her favorite way to spend time was "working in my garden while my five A.S.P.C.A. dogs smell the roses … or water them."

A reporter once asked Fontaine how she would like to die. Her response sums up her view on life in her 90s: "At age 108, flying around the stage in Peter Pan, as a result of my sister cutting the wires. Olivia has always said I was first at everything—I got married first, got an Academy Award first, had a child first. If I die, she'll be furious, because again I'll have got there first!" On December 15, 2013, 96 year old Joan Fontaine died quietly in her sleep at her home in Carmel. Sure enough, she was survived by her older sister, Olivia de Havilland, who said she was "shocked and saddened" by her sister's death. When looking back over her long and full life, Fontaine once told a reporter, "Everybody has hard times and good times, in I think a kind of balance. I've had some very marvelous times, and therefore I have to have the other one too, equally I just don't want it all in the middle. I would hate to just travel in middle gear for the rest of my life." It's certainly fair to say she was rarely ever in middle gear.

Bibliography

Beeman, Marsha Lynn. *Joan Fontaine: A Bio-Bibliography*. Westport, Connecticut: Greenwood, 1994.

De Havilland, Olivia. *Every Frenchman Has One*. New York: Random House, 1962.

Fontaine, Joan. *No Bed of Roses: An Autobiography*. New York: William Morrow and Company, 1978.

Higham, Charles. *Sisters: The Story of Olivia De Havilland and Joan Fontaine*. New York: Coward McCann, 1984.

Quinlan, David. *Quinlan's Film Stars.* London: B.T. Batsford Ltd, 1996.

Printed in Great Britain
by Amazon